# when the lights
# go out

## Other books by Graham Cooke

*Crafted Prayer*
*Developing Your Prophetic Gifting*
*A Divine Confrontation*
*Drawing Close*
*God Revealed*
*The Language of Love*
*The Secret of a Powerful Inner Life*

# when the lights go out

## go out

*Surprising Growth When God Is Hidden*

being with God series

## Graham Cooke

**Chosen**
Grand Rapids, Michigan

Published by Chosen Books
A division of Baker Publishing Group
P.O. Box 6287, Grand Rapids, MI 49516-6287
www.chosenbooks.com

Originally published under the title *Hiddenness and Manifestation*
by Sovereign World Limited of Tonbridge, Kent, England

Printed in the United States of America

Library of Congress Cataloging-in-Publication Data is on file at the
Library of Congress, Washington, D.C.

ISBN 0-8007-9383-8

Scripture is taken from the New King James Version. Copyright ©
1982 by Thomas Nelson, Inc. Used by permission. All rights
reserved.

There is only one Person I can dedicate this book to—the Holy Spirit. I am constantly amazed at His wisdom, revelation and power in my life. I love His dedication to, and His passion for, the Lord Jesus Christ. The way He reveals the Son to me has changed my life. His physical, emotional, mental and spiritual representation of the Father to me has continuously made me more excited and in awe of the great love of God for me.

# contents

# acknowledgments

Heather, Ben with Sioux, Seth and Yvonne and, of course, Sophie: What a great, wacky family we are ... I love it!

Carole Shiers, my personal assistant and faithful ministry partner for many, many years: Thank you.

To the respective churches in Southampton (UK) and Vacaville (USA) that I call home: Thank you, especially to my leaders, Billy and Caroline Kennedy (UK) and David and Deborah Crone (USA) for including us and being our friends.

To Tim and Darlene Dickerson who graciously provide a home, support, and, above all, true, loving friendship that withholds nothing: What a great blessing our relationship is for me and my family.

To Jordan Bateman, thank you for helping me enormously with the journal project, and to Tim Pettingale, my publisher and friend, whose passion for books and the written word is only outdone by his love for Jesus.

Finally, to the man in the coffee house who started this journey and to Peter Hocken who confirmed its rightness.

# introduction

It was just a normal Tuesday in the UK. Rain fell
from gray skies. A mirror image of my own soul—
dark, depressing, melancholic.

I was sitting in a coffee shop with no answers to
pressing needs of faith and spirituality. So many
questions, so little revelation and an experience of
God sadly lacking in favor or power. Where was He
when I needed Him most? Only my perverse
stubbornness kept me clinging to hope. For the
thousand-and-first time, my only prayer for my life
left my heart and fluttered heavenward like a timid
butterfly on wings of gossamer.

The coffee-shop door opened and in walked a
man. The place was full. He looked around and
caught my eye. Wearily, I gestured to the only seat
available at my table. Ordering coffee, we fell into a
desultory conversation: name, what do you do? etc.
He was a Catholic priest, Father whatever … I still
can't remember. I asked him about my current

agonizing question that had been exercising my soul for months: "What do you do when God is far away and you can't feel His presence?"

I remember his smile, but not his face. We spoke for over two hours. At least he spoke—I sat mesmerized. The coffee shop closed around us, so we moved into his car in the rain. His words changed my whole perspective in the spiritual realm. Later, after he had left, I had perfect recall and wrote steadily for three hours.

I'm a changed man through that conversation. I have learned to have a conversation with God in a new way.

I have developed a whole new perception of spiritual reality and a language to go with it. The man, Father Whatshisname, taught me about *hiddenness and manifestation.*

He left no forwarding address, but I'll be seeing him again ... one day.

# when the lights go out

At certain times in life, we feel the presence of God very tangibly. Our whole life seems touched by His presence, and we freely enjoy being with Him. At other times, God seems to be distant or even absent. We don't feel His presence in the same way as we did—maybe not at all. We don't experience the sense of peace and well-being that we enjoyed before. Why is this? Is it normal? Is it because we have done something wrong?

I believe the answer lies in understanding the ways of God more fully and deeply, and learning to live accordingly. This book focuses on the area of *hiddenness and manifestation* and seeks to help the reader discern these "seasons" of the ways of God. Living within the flow of these seasons is a critical spiritual discipline to learn. Once you understand them and learn to flow with them, you will enjoy a real sense of freedom and will not be buffeted by emotions or circumstances as you once were.

*Manifestation* describes the times when you feel God's presence and His touch upon your life in a very immediate way. He is just *there*! Those times are wonderful and effortless. But God also brings seasons of *hiddenness* into your life, and although He is still very much with you, you don't feel His presence in the same way. It seems at times that God strips away all the external paraphernalia of your life and denies it to you. At those times, you have to *believe* that you have peace with God, because you don't feel it in your emotions.

> "Manifestation" is about experiencing all that God is doing. "Hiddenness" is about possessing the things of God through His Word by faith.

*Manifestation* is about experiencing all that God is doing. *Hiddenness* is about possessing the things of God through His Word by faith. During times of hiddenness, you must learn to rely on the promises that God has made to you through the Bible.

## manifestation is a time of blessing and hiddenness is a time of building

Perhaps the simplest way to explain it is to say that manifestation is a time of *blessing*; hiddenness is a time of *building*. God desires to bring you through seasons of hiddenness because He wants you to learn the discipline of walking by the Spirit.

Developing an ongoing walk with God by the power of the Holy Spirit is a discipline. Practicing faith is a discipline. Hiddenness is God's way of establishing these disciplines in your life. Once established, they prevent the enemy from invading your life and touching you, because regardless of your emotions, you know how to find the presence of God; you have a constant assurance of His presence and His commitment to you.

Understanding the fact that sometimes God is hidden and sometimes manifest will ground you in your faith and help you to have a more consistent walk with Him. Whether it's a "good" day or a "bad" day, you will know how to live in the grace of God. Some days you will feel very close to God, and other days you won't—but it won't matter, because you will know that you can live, enjoying God's presence when you feel it, and enjoying living in your faith when you don't.

## hiddenness connects us with God's wisdom

Hiddenness connects us with God's wisdom, and wisdom is the revelation of who God is and the internal recognition of how He likes to work in our lives. Faith depends upon one thing—your understanding of the nature of God. Faith that is grounded in a sure understanding of the nature of God and what He is like will never be short of things for which to believe. You know what God is like, you know that He is faithful, that He'll never leave you or forsake you, that He's made provision for you, you know God never changes ... and so on.

> Wisdom is the revelation of who God is and the internal recognition of how He likes to work in our lives.

Faith in the nature of God is what keeps you moving even when situations are against you. Because you know that God is faithful, when a situation seems bleak or even impossible, you know just enough to wait for Him to come to your aid. *I know You, Lord. You're here somewhere. I'm just going to wait until You come or wait until You speak. I know You're doing something. I haven't figured out what it is yet, but I'm just going to wait because I know You.*

## real wisdom is hidden

"From where then does wisdom come?
And where is the place of understanding?
It is hidden from the eyes of all living."

Job 28:20–21

Real wisdom is hidden from us until God reveals it
to us. He often chooses to do that in the place of
hiddenness. Hiddenness is God's training ground.
In hiddenness God is teaching us the wisdom of
how to walk with Him, how to know Him, how to
understand Him and how to live a life of reverent
fear. David said, "Behold, You desire truth in the
inward parts, And in the hidden part You will make
me to know wisdom" (Psalm 51:6), because he
understood that eventually hiddenness and wisdom
are related. Likewise, Paul said:

> However, we speak wisdom among those who are
> mature, yet not the wisdom of this age, nor of the
> rulers of this age, who are coming to nothing. But
> we speak the wisdom of God in a mystery, the
> hidden wisdom which God ordained before the ages
> for our glory.
>
> 1 Corinthians 2:6–7

In times of manifestation, we cannot hear deep
truth. If we do hear God speak while we are
enjoying a season of His blessing, often we don't
understand what He is saying. Times of
manifestation are about *experiencing* God. They
are about moving in His flow—participating in the

peace, joy and life of God. Hiddenness is a different thing altogether—it is about understanding the deep things of God.

## hiddenness is where we process deep truth

> Then He took the twelve aside and said to them, "Behold, we are going up to Jerusalem, and all things that are written by the prophets concerning the Son of Man will be accomplished. For He will be delivered to the Gentiles and will be mocked and insulted and spit upon. They will scourge Him and kill Him. And the third day He will rise again." But they understood none of these things; this saying was hidden from them, and they did not know the things which were spoken.
>
> Luke 18:31–34

After Jesus' death, burial and resurrection, suddenly things began to come clear for His disciples. Much of what He had told them while they were enjoying His presence, they had not understood. When they saw Him, resurrected and standing once again in their midst, however, numerous things He had said flooded back to them, and suddenly they made sense. A time of manifestation is not a time to understand deep truth, but to experience God, which is what He wants for us. Hiddenness is where we start to process deep truth.

## hiddenness develops the inner man of the spirit

In our Christian lives, it is the Holy Sprit who promotes the internal development of our "inner man"—our spirit. We don't gain spiritual maturity by accumulating knowledge, but by increasing in godly wisdom. This kind of wisdom comes from above and cannot be gained by academic study. James 3 tells us that there are two kinds of wisdom— one is earthly and natural. Often this kind of wisdom appears to have some merit, but it is usually rooted in the value systems of the world. If we take too much notice of this kind of wisdom, it can lead us into a place where we become vulnerable to demonic influence as we become philosophical about our beliefs. By contrast, the supernatural wisdom to which James refers is pure, peaceable, gentle, reasonable, full of mercy and good fruit and unwavering in its convictions about God.

You will increase in this "supernatural" wisdom as you learn to be with God in hiddenness. The wisdom you gain from this experience can give you a whole new perspective on situations in your life. It will produce in you a rest and a peace that, frankly, will be astonishing to you.

There is an intriguing verse in Revelation 2 in which Jesus says, "To him who overcomes I will give some of the hidden manna to eat" (Revelation 2:17).

What I find interesting about this particular verse is that it was spoken to a church in Pergamos, which was situated in the middle of occult territory. The leaders had deliberately planted a church in the center of a demonic stronghold. How's that for bravery! They had picked the darkest place they could find to plant their church.

> In the time of greatest persecution, they would know how to live in the secret place of God.

Other Christians had been martyred there, and there was tremendous opposition to the Gospel. Yet, despite the constant persecution they suffered, God spoke to them of "hidden manna." This was their "inheritance word," if you like—that in the time of greatest persecution, they would know how to live in the secret place of God. He would provide *additional revelation* for them—hidden manna.

It is significant to note that God did not aim to take away the oppression, but to provide more revelation. Why? Because if we are going to learn to be overcomers, then we must allow ourselves to be developed *internally*. God is more interested in the state of our inner man than our outward circumstances. The hiddenness of God is all about that internal development. In times of manifestation, we focus outwardly on God and the blessings He showers on our lives. In hiddenness, we devote ourselves inwardly to God, yielding to Him in the things that He wants to do in our lives. The Lord wants each one of us to be able to live from the *inside out*, and to fully understand the process of internal development in Him.

## learning to live inwardly

In manifestation, we revel in our experience of the presence of God, and we are surrounded by Him. We hear His voice; we're touched by Him; there's lightness in our spirit, a joy in His presence. There's a strength, an ease in worship and prayer in times like that. The love of God fills us, and there's a release of His anointing. There's an enjoyment of God—His favor. God loves to show Himself to us in those times and seasons.

In hiddenness, God is still there, but He's hiding Himself because He wants to teach us a different way of living—one that does not depend upon our *experience* of Him. Now we have something much deeper by which to process our lives. He removes the visible in order to teach us to walk by faith, not by sight; to teach us how to live inwardly.

I believe that it is hiddenness that establishes our capacity to *rest* in the Lord. Hiddenness promotes a "quietness of soul"—our mind and emotions stilled before God. We have to learn how to submit our emotions to the discipline of life in the Spirit. To be able to bring yourself to a place of peace is an important discipline to have. Although it takes some time to learn, it is possible to develop it to the extent that you can bring yourself to a place of peace within a few seconds, regardless of the circumstances affecting you. It's just a discipline. It's no different from learning to drive a car or use a washing machine.

It is evident from the Scriptures that God has used this strategy of hiddenness for a long time. Early on in the Old Testament, we see it in His dealings with Jacob: "Then Jacob awoke from his sleep and said, 'Surely the LORD is in this place, and I did not know it'" (Genesis 28:16).

Here we see *retrospective revelation*, in other words, looking back and realizing that God was

## Ebb and Flow

Beloved one, see yourself in the Spirit.
Do you not know that you are in no way tied to just the
   natural world?

There is an old and limitless power available to you as you learn
   to step back into your inner man of the Spirit.
This anointing is like the creative operation of the ocean.
Wave after wave of revelation, power and anointing will wash
   over you as you learn to stand in the right place.

This place in the Spirit demands a transparency of honesty and
   a purity of heart.
I will help you to lower your resistance to the work of the
   Holy Spirit.

This is the dawn of a new season in your life, where the Son
   will rise upon you with a new warmth and light.
What now may be possible for you? What dreams long buried
   in your heart may surface to receive faith and recognition?
What now may emerge in your relationship with Me that will
   bring you into an increased significance in the Spirit?

Come away from the natural as you learn to be My bride,
My beauty, My love.

there. It's okay to live there, but what God really wants is *progressive revelation*—in which we trust that He is with us whether He is "visible" or not. That's the training that working within hiddenness can give you. It provides you with the ability to recognize God *when He is present,* not after the event.

## the disciples on the road to Emmaus

There is a classic example of hiddenness and manifestation exemplified throughout Luke 24. This passage of Scripture provides us with a number of clues as to why God would choose to move in hiddenness. Examining these in more detail will help us understand the extent of what God wants to do in each of our lives. Beginning at verse 13 we read:

> Now behold, two of them were traveling that same day to a village called Emmaus, which was seven miles from Jerusalem. And they talked together of all these things which had happened. So it was, while they conversed and reasoned, that Jesus Himself drew near and went with them. But their eyes were restrained, so that they did not know Him.

And He said to them, "What kind of conversation is this that you have with one another as you walk and are sad?"

Then the one whose name was Cleopas answered and said to Him, "Are You the only stranger in Jerusalem, and have You not known the things which happened there in these days?"

And He said to them, "What things?"

So they said to Him, "The things concerning Jesus of Nazareth, who was a Prophet mighty in deed and word before God and all the people, and how the chief priests and our rulers delivered Him to be condemned to death, and crucified Him. But we were hoping that it was He who was going to redeem Israel. Indeed, besides all this, today is the third day since these things happened. Yes, and certain women of our company, who arrived at the tomb early, astonished us. When they did not find His body, they came saying that they had also seen a vision of angels who said He was alive. And certain of those who were with us went to the tomb and found it just as the women had said; but Him they did not see."

Then He said to them, "O foolish ones, and slow of heart to believe in all that the prophets have spoken! Ought not the Christ to have suffered these things and to enter into His glory?" And beginning at Moses and all the Prophets, He expounded to them in all the Scriptures the things concerning Himself.

Then they drew near to the village where they were going, and He indicated that He would have gone farther. But they constrained Him, saying, "Abide with us, for it is toward evening, and the day is far spent." And He went in to stay with them.

Now it came to pass, as He sat at the table with them, that He took bread, blessed and broke it, and gave it to them. Then their eyes were opened and they knew Him; and He vanished from their sight.

And they said to one another, "Did not our heart burn within us while He talked with us on the road, and while He opened the Scriptures to us?" So they rose up that very hour and returned to Jerusalem, and found the eleven and those who were with them gathered together, saying, "The Lord is risen indeed, and has appeared to Simon!" And they told about the things that had happened on the road, and how He was known to them in the breaking of bread.

Luke 24:13–35

### Present but not visible
Jesus was *with* the disciples, but their eyes were prevented from seeing Him. *Hiddenness.* God hides for a reason—so that He can develop you on the

inside and train you to see with the eyes of faith. In manifestation, you can already see what God is doing. In hiddenness, you learn to look inward and recognize that God is still at work, relying purely on your faith.

## In hiddenness, God helps us to have a right perspective

One of the reasons for hiddenness is that God wants to help us clarify our thoughts and come to the right spiritual perspective. These two disciples were talking to each other on the road to Emmaus, trying to understand everything that had been happening. Sometimes as Christians we have endless discussions with no revelatory breakthrough. Usually, the result of endless discussion is to come full circle and arrive back at your starting point. You are still confused, and you still don't understand. The discussion has not taken you anywhere. The disciples were at this point. For all their debate, they had no true spiritual perspective from which they could process the events that were taking place. In such a case, God's hiddenness is what helps us to get back "on the level" in the Spirit—to process the circumstances from the point of view of faith and come to a place of peace. It is not essential that we *understand everything*, but that we *trust* God *in everything*.

If you are always seeking to be in a "manifest" relationship with God, then when the times of hiddenness come, you will only ever have a superficial understanding of what is going on in the spiritual realm. We have to dig for truth, and sometimes we try to understand things with our natural minds, with our human reasoning. In general, the only time God will speak to your mind is when you have sinned, when He says, "Come now, let us reason together." The rest of the time He says, "Don't lean on your own understanding; trust Me."

Before we open our minds to think through an event or circumstance that is troubling us, it is helpful to come to a place of worship: to set the problem aside and just focus on worshiping God. The place of worship is the place of trust and faith in God's presence. In the midst of our worship, we are renewed in spirit and mind and can more easily access a deeper level of spiritual wisdom. Because the disciples had no true supernatural perspective to help them process what was happening, they were bound to arrive at some kind of "soulish" analysis of the situation. A soulish, or purely emotional, analysis of events will usually lead you to become sad and downhearted because you can't understand why these things are so. *I'm confused. Why has this happened? I thought God was doing something here, but I don't understand it.* When you reach this place, it is then easy to begin blaming the enemy, assuming it to be an attack. We think, *It must be the enemy trying to confuse me and stop me from understanding.* Yet it's not the enemy, it's just God saying, *Listen, this is how I like to work. I want you to learn how to live from the inside.* We need to learn how to turn inward to find out what God is actually doing at this point in time.

Being sad and downhearted is one of the signs that people are not processing their hiddenness in cooperation with the Holy Spirit. Yet it's interesting that our sadness does not deflect the Lord from *His* objective: to develop our inner man. Often we are sad in times of hiddenness until we learn how to process it properly. Then, we learn how to rejoice in God from the inside to the outside, because we know that God is faithful and He is always working.

### Deep truth revealed

Through hiddenness, God seeks to uncover our wrong perspectives and bring us face to face with them. We find in verse 18 that the disciples had a perception of what had been happening during this whole season in Jerusalem. They spoke of Jesus the Nazarene who was a prophet. They said nothing about His being the Son of God, but instead reverted to type. They talked about how He was a prophet, mighty in deed and word in the sight of God, and how He was delivered up to the sentence of death and crucified.

This was the "soulish" perspective on who Jesus was and what had happened to Him. It was a conclusion to which any onlooker, not even a disciple, might have come. In the midst of the shock of Jesus' death, the disciples were processing the "facts" on a purely human level, with no insight into the spiritual realm. God uses hiddenness, therefore, to shed light on our ignorance and inform us about what He is really doing. He reveals the deeper truths to us that are imperceptible on the surface. One way in which God does this is to come and ask us questions. The questions are asked not because God is in need of information from us, but because they uncover things that we had not perceived.

**God doesn't always work in expected ways**
Sometimes we are convinced that we know what's going on, and God has to break through our

ignorance. Often that will make us feel slightly worse about a situation, until we stop pretending we know everything and go to God for help. When we simply come to God, humble ourselves and pray, *Father, I haven't a clue what's going on. Would You just let me in on what You're doing? It would be really helpful*, we reach a place of incredible liberty and peace.

Hiddenness helps us to process our own disappointment with God, because if we're honest, we sometimes have a perception of how God *should* be, how things *should* work and what He *should* be doing. When things don't happen the way we expect, we live with a sense of disappointment that maybe God has, in some way, let us down. The disciples said to one another, "We were hoping that it was He who was going to redeem Israel." They had an expectation of God that He had no intention of fulfilling at that time. I wonder how many of us are living with an expectation of God that He has no desire or intention to fulfill in our life, because our expectation is flawed. Often our hopes and expectations about God are built on very shaky thinking and need to be pulled down. Hiddenness

> Hiddenness will pull down the things that shouldn't be there.

will pull down the things that shouldn't be there.
That's part of the dynamic of it. Jesus overturned
several major expectations to which the Jewish
people, in general, were clinging:

1.  First, regarding the manner of His coming,
    Jesus came as a servant, not as a king. That
    didn't compute with the Jews' view of the
    Messiah. The fact that He came as a servant,
    born in a stable in inauspicious circumstances
    didn't square with their thinking, and so they
    ruled out the possibility that He was the
    Messiah. In their eyes, He had disqualified
    Himself by the manner of His coming.
2.  Second, He disappointed them in the sense
    of *for whom He came.* Jesus didn't just come
    to save the Jews; He came to save the
    Gentiles as well—everybody, in fact. This
    radically shook the Jewish thinking about
    the Messiah.
3.  Third, the Jews misunderstood the Messiah's
    main purpose—to establish a spiritual kingdom,
    not to rescue Israel from the Romans. The Jews
    viewed the Messiah as someone who would
    deliver Israel, but He never had any intention of
    *physically* doing that.

Jesus overturned all of the major expectations of the Jewish people, which is why so many of them failed to receive Him as the Messiah. The Scriptures reveal just how deeply ingrained in the Jewish mindset these expectations were. After Jesus' resurrection, having spent forty days teaching and just being with His disciples, they still asked Him the question, "Is this the time You're restoring the kingdom to Israel?" They still didn't yet fully understand for what He had come and what He was doing.

Because Jesus had no desire or intention to fulfill the expectations of the Jews, they missed Him. Likewise, we often miss what God is really doing because of our false expectations. It is a work of the enemy to sow such unrealistic expectations in our hearts. What God does in hiddenness is to process our disillusionment, from the inside to the outside in order to get rid of it. Hiddenness is always about a change of heart toward God, which in turn provokes a change of heart toward the people around us.

### Information versus revelation
Hiddenness will also expose your unbelief. In Luke 24:22, the disciples said, "Some women among us amazed us when they were at the tomb early in the morning. They didn't find Jesus' body. They came to

us saying that they had also seen a vision of angels who spoke to them, saying that Jesus was alive. Some of those who were with us went to the tomb and found it exactly as the women had said, but they didn't see Him—they didn't see anything."

The disciples had received some clues from the women regarding Jesus' resurrection, but they were still somewhat unconvinced. Maybe it was their prejudice against women that prevented them from believing. Who knows? Maybe they thought it was too good to be true. Maybe they were too "cerebral" in their approach to what was happening. In such situations, we have to learn the difference between *information* and *revelation*. You cannot receive revelation in your mind. Our minds can only receive information and process logic. You receive revelation in your spirit, and the vehicle that takes that revelation from your spirit into your conscious mind is faith.

> A relationship with God is an affair of the heart.

Revelation is a spiritual thing, because a relationship with God is an affair of the heart. Your heart receives truth to which your mind is then exposed. When you are "renewed in the spirit of your mind" about what God is saying to you, then you see it on a totally different level.

## In hiddenness, God answers our questions and teaches us His ways

Revelation, which is received in the heart, initially may offend the mind. Maybe that is what happened with the disciples. What they had heard regarding Jesus' resurrection didn't sound logical or reasonable. But God wanted them to get beyond the logic and see the truth He was revealing to their hearts. As we believe what God is saying to our hearts, our minds then make the adjustment, and so we're renewed in the spirit of our minds. In times of hiddenness, God begins to answer the questions buried deep in our hearts and to instruct us in His ways and thoughts. That is why Jesus began to expound on the Scriptures to the two disciples and reveal the truth.

Often we want physical, emotional or mental stimuli to help us process events, but revelation is born into the spirit man. Until we learn to live from our spirit, we will always be processing life from the soul, from our mind, emotions and will. Yet so often our thinking is defective or confused, and our emotions fluctuate from one extreme to another. When we are unsettled like this in our emotions, then we must learn how to consciously "retreat" into the inner man of the spirit in order to get our focus back upon God. We do that through worship, prayers of submission and an inner yielding, and by turning to the heart of God through sheer obedience using our will. The submission of our will to God through obedience is the entry point to the spiritual realm.

If you find submitting your will to God difficult, you can come before Him and ask for help. When you turn your will over to Him, He can then work in you to bring you to the place where He wants you to be (see Philippians 2:13). When God's desire and your desire match up, He is then released to work in you and through you. Hiddenness, then, is a major part of enabling you to partner with the Holy Spirit in what God is doing.

> When God's desire and your desire match up, He is then released to work in you and through you.

If you don't know or understand something, go straight to a place of rest and trust and wait for God in worship. It's just a discipline—you can do it. The Holy Spirit will begin to come and take hold of you. If you let your mind loose on the problem first, you'll only process things from your point of ignorance. If your spirit gets hold of the problem, however, then you will release faith toward God. Some people believe that God is not at work until they see some manifestation of His power. They don't "see" anything happening and so are fooled into believing that God is not at work. So it was with the Emmaus disciples. They didn't understand everything until they saw Him, and then it was, *Oh . . . I see!* Enter the "Oh . . . " factor: *Oh, right, I understand now.*

If this is where you are at in your relationship with God, it's okay. It's not wrong to be there, but don't stay there for long, because that's not the goal of spiritual maturity. Our aim should be to reach the place where we have the "Oh . . . " factor in our present circumstances—those that are affecting us right now—so that we can relax and trust that God is at work in our lives *now*. That is a much more powerful place in which to be, and the best reason to be there is because God wants it; it is His chosen way of deepening our relationship with Him.

You'll find in hiddenness that God always talks about Himself and reveals Himself in those times. Jesus began to talk to the disciples, expounding on the subject of the cross and how it can be seen all throughout the Scriptures, in order to teach them about Himself. In hiddenness, God loves to tell you all about Himself, but He wants to have you *all to Himself* to do it. As you learn the discipline of retreating into your spirit, you will find that God is actually extremely communicative. He loves to share things with us, but He wants to do it in a particular place in a particular way. Most of my understanding about the nature of God—His kindness, goodness and mercy—has come to me in times of hiddenness, when God has just spoken to me, telling me and convincing me of who He is and what He's really like.

**In hiddenness, God always wants to go farther than we do**

In Luke 24 we read, "[Jesus] indicated that He would have gone farther. But they constrained Him, saying, 'Abide with us, for it is toward evening, and the day is far spent.' And He went in to stay with them" (Luke 24:28–29).

I think there was more that Jesus wanted to share with the disciples about Himself—more revelation that would probably have brought them into a deeper understanding of truth, but they urged Him to stay. It was as if they had reached their limit and couldn't absorb any more revelation for a while. Jesus actually graciously consented to stay with them. I believe that if our capacity to enjoy hiddenness is limited, then our experience and understanding of God will be limited by the same measure. You should stay in hiddenness until God pushes you out. Jesus would have gone farther, but the disciples were not capable. In fact, Jesus said to His disciples, "I still have many things to say to you, but you cannot bear them now" (John 16:12).

It is interesting that in hiddenness God always wants to go farther than we do. We need to learn to stay in the place of hiddenness, in God's presence, until we receive everything that God has for us during that time. It is easy to break off from hiddenness too soon. In our hearts we may secretly feel that manifestation is the ultimate thing, and that hiddenness is second best. In reality, there is no difference between the two—they are both brilliant! You just

> God always wants to go that extra mile, and He wants to take us with Him.

need to learn to live in them both. God always wants to go that extra mile, and He wants to take us with Him. There is a discipline attached to being hidden with God, and you have to learn the joy of that discipline, staying there until God moves you on. He will often do this by bringing you into manifestation, but if you move on before God tells you to, then you will miss something. Don't push just for experience—stay hidden until God says it's time to move on. When we become comfortable with the ways of God in hiddenness, we will find ourselves going farther in the realm of the Spirit than ever before. We'll go farther than we ever thought possible in our present circumstances, because He'll take us to a place of deeper revelation, and we will experience a bigger breakthrough.

I believe that Jesus revealed His identity prematurely to His disciples, because they were in danger of totally missing the point of what He was saying. Sometimes our desire for manifestation and blessing can reduce our capacity to be nurtured in the spiritual realm, and we'll miss something. Jesus must have decided that they had reached their capacity in terms of the revelation that He could impart to them and so suddenly He revealed Himself and they began rejoicing: "Now it came to pass, as He sat at the table with them, that He took bread, blessed and broke it, and gave it to them. Then their eyes were opened and they knew Him; and He vanished from their sight" (Luke 24:30–31).

Everything was much clearer now in the disciples' thinking and perception. Their eyes had been opened, everything had come into focus and they couldn't wait to share the truth with other people. But Jesus vanished as soon as He had manifested Himself to them.

I believe He vanished because the disciples did not
have the maturity to walk with Him in that place.
They could have experienced more—I think God was
certainly willing—but they were unable to receive it.

As God "builds up" your inner man with the
progressive revelation of who He is, you are
inevitably changed and transformed. You begin to
reflect those qualities of God's character that have
been revealed to you, and you become a living
testimony of what God is like. Because you know
that God is faithful, you become faithful by the word
He has given you. That is why Jesus said things like,
"Now you are clean through the word that I have
spoken to you," because the word that God gives
you in hiddenness takes hold of your life and
changes you.

## rest is a weapon

Every experience of God's manifestation in our lives
is a bonus. I am choosing to live my life in
hiddenness, so that when God's manifestation
comes, it's a bonus. I want to live in that place of
constantly yielding inwardly to find the presence of
God—the place that, even in the eye of the storm, is
one of tranquillity, of peace and of rest. In such a

place, "rest" becomes a weapon against the enemy. You can exasperate the devil, because when he comes against you, you don't fight against him, but submit to God (see James 4:7).

In fact, it is not our job to fight the devil. Our job is to "step back" into God and experience His majesty and power. Christ has overcome the devil, so we need to focus on being "in Christ." You never have to go looking for the devil. If you live "in Christ," he'll come and find you. Jesus never went looking for the devil. Everywhere He went, the devil appeared and tried to oppose Him. Our spiritual warfare, therefore, should not be about becoming preoccupied with the devil, but about becoming preoccupied with God. Real warfare is about discovering the majesty, the supremacy and the sovereignty of the Lord Jesus Christ. Warfare is about seeking the face of God and enjoying Him as your fortress and your refuge.

In the place of rest, hidden with God, He is able to reveal to us strategies to overcome in any situation. We see this in the life of King David, who constantly sought the Lord's direction, especially concerning battle strategies. When the Philistines came and spread themselves in the valley of Rephaim, David went to the Lord and asked, "Shall I go up against them?" (2 Samuel 5:19). He wasn't worried about what the Philistines were doing; he just got into the presence of God and said, "You're in control of this; what should I do?" The Lord said to him, "Go up directly." David did what the Lord told him, and so he won the battle. When the enemy came again into the valley of Rephaim, David sought the Lord again and asked, "Shall I go up directly against them?" He was basing his logic on his previous experience. It had worked last time, so perhaps it would work again. Sometimes referring to your experience is fine, but at other times, it's your experience that prevents you from getting the breakthrough. But relying on what you know can never be a substitute for getting revelation. David needed to ask the Lord, "Is there a new strategy, a new tactic You want me to use?"

In this instance, God said, "No, don't go directly up. Don't do what you did last time. Circle around behind them, and stand in the balsam trees, and when you hear the wind blowing in the tops of the trees, then go out, and you'll win." Often God has to employ totally different tactics in dealing with us because He doesn't want us to revert to relying on our experience. The only time you should rely on your experience is when God isn't saying anything new. If He doesn't give you any new tactics, that is His way of saying, "Do what you did last time." But you still need to come before God and ask, "Lord, what do You want to do in these circumstances?" This is all part of seeking refuge in His hiddenness and living in that fortress—the inner, secret place of the presence of God.

> The only time you should rely on your experience is when God isn't saying anything new.

## other examples of hiddenness and manifestation in the Scriptures

Scripture has many other examples of hiddenness and manifestation from which we can learn. In John 20, Mary was in the Garden of Gethsemane, grieving over the death of Jesus:

> Now when she had said this, she turned around and saw Jesus standing there, and did not know that it was Jesus. Jesus said to her, "Woman, why are you weeping? Whom are you seeking?"
> She, supposing Him to be the gardener, said to Him, "Sir, if You have carried Him away, tell me where You have laid Him, and I will take Him away."

Jesus said to her, "Mary!"

She turned and said to Him, "Rabboni!" (which is to say, Teacher).

John 20:14–16

It's always a personal moment with God that takes us from hiddenness to manifestation. For Mary, He just had to say her name, and suddenly that was it. At first she thought that Jesus was the gardener until He spoke her name; then she realized who He was. This switch from hiddenness to manifestation was intensely personal. It is often this way with God. In the context of friendship and fellowship, He speaks out your name, and suddenly everything is different.

In 2 Corinthians 12, Paul, who was being buffeted by the enemy, desperately wanted a manifestation of God's power to deliver him. But God wanted Paul in hiddenness, to experience His grace and to make Paul aware of his own weakness. God wanted Paul to be *kept.* That is a characteristic of hiddenness, being kept, and the experience brought Paul into a whole new realm of God's sovereignty. A whole new acquaintance with the majesty of God was born in Paul's life, and a whole new dimension of anointing came out of it. He emerged from that season with an understanding of the spiritual realm so deep that he could barely cope with it.

In Acts 10 we read about the revelation God gave to Peter in a vision detailing how He desired to reach out to the Gentiles. Peter did not understand what was going on, but after some persuasion, he simply obeyed God:

> The next day ... Peter went up on the housetop to pray, about the sixth hour. Then he became very hungry and wanted to eat; but while they made ready, he fell into a trance and saw heaven opened and an object like a great sheet bound at the four corners, descending to him and let down to the earth. In it were all kinds of four-footed animals of the earth, wild beasts, creeping things, and birds of the air. And a voice came to him, "Rise, Peter; kill and eat."
>
> But Peter said, "Not so, Lord! For I have never eaten anything common or unclean."
>
> And a voice spoke to him again the second time, "What God has cleansed you must not call common." This was done three times. And the object was taken up into heaven again.
>
> Now while Peter wondered within himself what this vision which he had seen meant, behold, the men who had been sent from Cornelius had made inquiry for Simon's house, and stood before the

gate. And they called and asked whether Simon,
whose surname was Peter, was lodging there.

While Peter thought about the vision, the Spirit
said to him, "Behold, three men are seeking you.
Arise therefore, go down and go with them,
doubting nothing; for I have sent them."

Acts 10:9-20

Peter had the vision three times—a sheet lowered
down from heaven full of creepy crawlies and a voice
saying, "Arise, Peter; kill and eat." Peter's immediate
reaction to the Lord was, "That's not *kosher*—we
don't do this sort of stuff, Lord. You wrote the book,
remember?" He was perplexed. Sometimes when we
are in hiddenness we are confused and uncertain.
But Peter obeyed God, and he went, even with his
reservations. God had told him, "Arise and go,
without misgiving." Although Peter had many
concerns about what he was being told to do,
nevertheless, he went in obedience and entered the
house of the Gentiles. At that moment, he also
entered the realm of spiritual insight. He said, "I
perceive now that God is no respecter of persons."

Then Peter opened his mouth and said: "In truth I
perceive that God shows no partiality. But in every

nation whoever fears Him and works righteousness
is accepted by Him."

Acts 10:34–35

It should not be underestimated what a momentous
occasion this was for Peter. In a moment, his entire
mindset of ministry changed as the inclusion of the
Gentiles in all that God was doing came sharply into

focus. I believe it was God's way of
dealing with Peter's prejudice and
racism, because there seems to be no
doubt that Peter was a racist. He
would say one thing to the Jews and
a different thing to the Gentiles. God
was healing and delivering him from that mindset.
In hiddenness and manifestation, being perplexed
and learning to perceive things differently are key
learning points. It's okay to be perplexed, so long as
you're learning how to perceive spiritual realities on
a different level.

> In hiddenness and manifestation, being perplexed and learning to perceive things differently are key learning points.

## different reactions to hiddenness

The life of King David provides us with some good
examples of common reactions to hiddenness. Have
you ever asked yourself the question when you read

## Ring of Fire

My child, stay in Me. My ring of fire is your protection. Live in
    Me and rest.
As you learn to remain in the secret place of the Most High,
You will be invisible to the evil one.

When the clamor and pressure of warfare is great around you,
Know that it is just the enemy seeking to get you to break
    cover in panic.
Fear reveals where you are hiding.

Your place is to dwell, to rest, to stay and remain in the Secret
    Place of My Spirit.
It is an attitude of heart and mind combining to enable you to
    sit in transparent fellowship.
The more transparent your heart is before Me, the more obscure
    you are to the enemy.

When the evil one seeks to do his worst, you may relax in Me as
    I do My best!

the Psalms, *Why did David go through so many similar experiences?* Simply put, it's because he kept failing his tests. Why did he constantly return to the same themes throughout the Psalms? Because God was trying to get this "thicko" to learn how to live in the Spirit! David spoke of the same experiences over and over again, until he finally learned how to walk with God. He frequently misunderstood God in times of hiddenness and sometimes even thought that God had totally rejected him.

**"God has forgotten me."**
Hence in Psalm 44, David said:

> Why do You hide Your face,
> And forget our affliction and our oppression?
> Arise for our help,
> And redeem us for Your mercies' sake.
>
> verses 24, 26

On the surface, this seems like a good prayer, but underlying it is actually a very soulish reaction. It's a prayer asking for manifestation in a time of hiddenness. David cries out, "God, You've forgotten about me!" He completely missed the point of what God was trying to do in him.

"God has rejected me."
Similarly, in Psalm 88, David said: "LORD, why do
You cast off my soul? Why do You hide Your face
from me?" (verse 14).

Initially, David saw the whole idea of hiddenness
as *rejection*, thinking that God had had enough of
him and had cast him away.

**"God is angry with me."**
In Psalm 89, David said:

> How long, LORD?
> Will You hide Yourself forever?
> Will Your wrath burn like fire?
> Remember how short my time is [I'm running out of
>         time here, God—do something!];
> For what futility have You created all the children
>         of men?
> What man can live and not see death?
> Can he deliver his life from the power of the grave?
> Selah
> Lord, where are Your former lovingkindnesses,
> Which You swore to David in Your truth?
> Remember, Lord, the reproach of Your servants—
> How I bear in my bosom the reproach of all the
>         many peoples,
> With which Your enemies have reproached, O LORD,

> With which they have reproached the footsteps of
>     Your anointed.
> Blessed be the LORD forevermore!
> Amen and Amen.
>
> verses 46–52

Again, all of this sounds quite spiritual, but it isn't!
It's very soulish. David is pouring out his emotions
and missing the point. In verses 50–51, he is trying
to justify his prayer of restoration, which gives you
a clue to his mindset—he just wants to be delivered
and set free. It seems like a good prayer, but he is
trying to escape the purposeful time of hiddenness
into which God has led him. David puts the whole
process down to the *wrath of God. God is angry with
me for some reason*, he thought. *That's why this is
happening to me.*

**"God is punishing me because of some sin."**
Job had a similar problem to David. In Job 13, we
hear the plea: "Why do You hide Your face, And
regard me as Your enemy?" (Job 13:24).

All Job can see at that moment is his own
situation. He cannot yet see the hand of God, so he
mistakes everything as God's wrath. This is probably
the most common mistake that people make—to

think that hiddenness, the lack of God's tangible presence, occurs because He is angry with us for some reason. We usually assume that He is angry because we have, either knowingly or unknowingly, committed some terrible sin. There are rare occasions when God hides His face because of sin, but this is not generally the reason for His hiddenness. The prophet Isaiah did make mention of such occasions, however: "You have hidden Your face from us, And have consumed us because of our iniquities" (Isaiah 64:7).

> For the iniquity of his covetousness
> I was angry and struck him;
> I hid and was angry,
> And he went on backsliding in the way of his heart.
>
> Isaiah 57:17

This is obviously not the case now in the light of the New Covenant in Christ. God punished Jesus for our sin and makes His grace available to us in Christ. Now we have confidence to enter the holy place by the blood of Jesus, by a new and living way (see Hebrews 10:19–20).

Because of that, we can draw near with confidence to "the throne of grace, that we may obtain mercy and find grace to help in time of need" (Hebrews 4:16). That our sin is covered is part of the glorious good news of the Gospel.

**When God hides His face, people are dismayed.** In Psalm 104:29, David said, "You hide Your face, they are troubled...." This is a typically soulish response to hiddenness. God hides, and we "freak out." David continued by saying: "You take away their breath, they die and return to their dust. You send forth Your Spirit, they are created; And You renew the face of the earth" (Psalm 104:29-30).

In other words, when God hides His face in hiddenness, people are often dismayed—a typical reaction. Once we learn and understand God's seasons of hiddenness and manifestation, however, we will no longer be alarmed when He "hides His face."

David's best response is in Psalm 13:1-3, where he finally seems to understand what's going on:

> How long, O Lord? Will You forget me forever?
> How long will You hide Your face from me?
> How long shall I take counsel in my soul,
> Having sorrow in my heart daily?
> How long will my enemy be exalted over me?

Consider and hear me, O LORD my God;
Enlighten my eyes,
Lest I sleep the sleep of death.

Here David is finally beginning to track with God,
and he's praying for enlightenment in a time of
hiddenness. This is what the issue is really all
about. Don't assume anything—wait to hear from
God.

Isaiah had a great understanding of the process of
hiddenness, as prophets usually do. In Isaiah 8, he
wrote: "And I will wait on the LORD, Who hides His
face from the house of Jacob; And I will hope in
Him" (verse 17).

And again in chapter 45, he wrote: "Truly You are
God, who hide Yourself, O God of Israel, the Savior!"
(verse 15).

## the joy of hiddenness

I believe that hiddenness is one of the most exciting
disciplines that we can learn in the realm of the
Spirit. When you learn how to access it and live in
it, suddenly everything makes sense. Everything
falls to you. All the things that come against you
only enable you to go deeper into God, because you

have learned the discipline of living in His presence. A man involved in hiddenness, looking for meaning, is a delight to the Lord. Isaiah understood God's ways, and all his attention was upon God and what He would do.

> A man involved in hiddenness, looking for meaning, is a delight to the Lord.

Therefore, understanding hiddenness and manifestation will train us how to determine the "windows of the soul"—those moments when we perceive what is happening in the spiritual realm.

I believe that there is a wealth of revelation and understanding that God wants to pour into your spirit. Sometimes we become weary of struggling through the Christian life because we don't know how to replenish ourselves in the Spirit. The discipline of hiddenness will enable you to recover, restore your soul, renew your mind and refresh your spirit. For me, coming into that place of hiddenness has been one of my greatest joys and blessings, and one of the reasons why, to a degree, I've perfected the art of "bouncing back" in life. I know that I can defeat the devil by ignoring him, by retreating into my spirit and just doing business with God. Living in that place where God wants us to be, no matter what the enemy throws at us, will only make us stronger. We come out of our hidden place with greater revelation than when we entered it. It is the key to the place of power and significance in the Spirit.

## hiddenness opens the door for abundant life

Understanding how God works through hiddenness and manifestation opens the door to a better way of life. It reveals to us the abundant life that Jesus promised: "The thief does not come except to steal, and to kill, and to destroy. I have come that they may have life, and that they may have it more abundantly" (John 10:10).

According to Jesus, there are two beings in the world, both dedicated to something extreme. One, the enemy, seeks our destruction. The devil hates us with a malignant, malevolent, malicious hatred. He wants to destroy us through lies, theft and murder. He hopes to extinguish everything we are, everything we have and everything we are destined to be.

The other being, God, wants to do the complete opposite. God wants to give us a life that is lavish and exuberant. He wants our being to teem with possibility and generosity. His form of life is so abundant and full that it actually lifts us to a place where the enemy cannot work. When He does that, we are not subject to the devil in any way, shape or form. The enemy becomes afraid of us—we begin to erode his ability to release poverty and degradation.

> God wants us to teem with possibility and generosity.

An abundant life is one that is dedicated to overthrowing the work of evil. It uses the antidote of faith in who God is to destroy the kingdom of darkness. "Do not be overcome by evil, but overcome evil with good," Paul said in Romans 12:21. What if the biggest problem in the world right now isn't terrorism? What if it's not the economy, drugs, hopelessness or sickness? What if the biggest problem in the world right now is simply a lack of goodness? I believe evil is rising around us because there is not enough goodness to keep it down.

When the people of God learn deep lessons about God through hiddenness, and then experience Him powerfully in manifestation, goodness is birthed in us. When we disparage or avoid either extreme, we don't fully discover who God is for us; goodness, then, cannot be produced in us in anything close to a full measure. And without that goodness, we cannot overcome evil.

## the Kingdom of heaven

The goal of the Kingdom of heaven is to produce people who really know how to live abundantly. These followers of Christ don't fear their economic situation, because they know God wants to be their provider. We are called to be a company of people on earth who know how to be loved by God. Our joy does not depend on an emotional event or stimulus— it depends on our revelation of who God is.

If such a company existed, the enemy would be stripped of his ability to wreak havoc and misery. The whole point of the Kingdom of heaven is to raise us to a place where we live far above the enemy's ability to damage us.

We can live this way now. The promise of eternal life does not come into effect when we die. Eternal life is given to us the instant we accept Christ as our Savior. If you are saved, you are living an eternal life right now. It has already begun.

We cannot have one kind of life here on earth and another in heaven: Such talk is doublemindedness. There is a quality of life here that matches the quality of life into which we will someday come. Our current journey enables us to live in the premise and the promise of such eternal life.

Anything less than complete abundance is not true life. Anything less than what Jesus died to give us cannot be termed as life as He wants it. Our mission is to pursue life as He understands it, not as we do.

Most Christians I have met are not living in anywhere near that kind of abundance. Some of this has to do with the mind games the devil plays with us. He has craftily convinced many Christians that the spiritual life is one of toil, pain, suffering and unbelievably miserable sacrifice. The enemy downgrades our understanding of our place in God's affection. He has "messed with our heads" and deceived the people of God into accepting a lower class of Christian life. It's as though we have a first-class ticket, but we are content to fly in a dog kennel in the belly of an airplane.

The enemy works day and night to bring us to a lower perception of ourselves and God. He loves ineffective, blasé Christians. He degrades our faith over and over and over again. He has developed a generation of secret cynics, people who don't fully trust the power of God or His provision.

The more religious and world-weary we become, the more static our faith is. We stop reaching out in faith to touch God. We become comfortable with

His hiddenness and stop bothering to look for what He is trying to teach us through those seasons. We quit asking the Father for anything, and we extinguish hope and faith. From there, it's a small step to self-reliance and ignoring God's provision or aid completely. We tolerate rather than confront.

This is what destruction looks like in the 21st-century Church: tired, defeated Christians living lives of silent desperation. People who come to meetings and conferences because they believe more in an event-oriented God than a lifestyle one. Our faith is bankrupt, and the world looks at us like a sales clerk looking at someone whose credit card has been rejected: "I'm sorry, your card has been declined. You've reached your credit limit."

Too many Christians are content to live a declined—a rejected, turned away, empty, unworthy, unable to receive—life. But in that place of dejection, a miracle can happen. Like the first flower poking through the cold ground of winter, God breathes on us: *I have come that you may have life, and that you may have it more abundantly.*

The Kingdom of heaven expands on earth when we become intimately acquainted with God and access Him through our one-on-one relationship with Him. When we walk with God in childlike simplicity, we learn everything we need to know to live this life fully.

## living in abundance

Living in the nature of God guarantees our abundance. Horticulturalists know the fruitfulness of a tree not by examining the branches—where the fruit actually grows—but by checking the health of the trunk. Separate a branch from a trunk and the branch dies. Likewise, we die when we are separated from the trunk of God's presence. We must learn how to remain connected to the trunk of God's nature during seasons of hiddenness and manifestation.

> Living in the nature of God guarantees our abundance.

It is abnormal for a branch that is connected to a healthy tree trunk to be unfruitful. Similarly, it is abnormal for a life lived in Jesus to be unhealthy. The problem exists between our ears: We need to be transformed in the way we see things and in the way we think. Our perception of God truly does drive everything about our life.

Everything about God wants to raise us up to be seated in heavenly places with Him. When we're with Him, we gain a completely different perspective of what is happening around us. We see a different landscape looking down from a mountain than we do looking up from a valley.

God loves us all absolutely, and we are worthy of that love. I know I am worthy of that love. I don't put such value on myself—God did by sending His Son to die for me. He declared that I was worth that price. So for me to say that I'm unworthy would mean I was spitting on Jesus' sacrifice. I don't want to do that. I am worthy of salvation.

We are transformed when we repent. Repentance means that we "think again." We had a thought, and it didn't take us anywhere, so now we have to think again. Many Christians need to rethink their commitment to being "unworthy." In fact, we are very worthy because God has made us that way.

We need to think of ourselves not as Christians, but as disciples of Christ. Christians seem content to be passive. But disciples—or followers—of Christ are wild men and women, unstoppable forces of nature. They bring the Kingdom of heaven to earth. They think how Jesus thinks. They speak how Jesus speaks. They do what Jesus does. They live an abundant, transformed life.

God wants to give us a heavenly mindset so that we can become a lot of earthly good. If we don't think like a heavenly citizen—if our mind is not fully renewed—we need to question from where our mindset actually comes. If we don't see the depths of who God is for us or understand the depths of His love for us, we have been deceived. When we buy into the enemy's lies, we become like a cloud without rain: We obscure heaven and don't give anything back to earth.

## an imaginative people

An active imagination is part of the DNA of God's people. When we are touched by the Holy Spirit, we are free to think creatively about God and ourselves. There should be nothing bland or boring about the Church of Jesus Christ. We should be colorful, exciting, imaginative people—an enigma that no one can solve. What if the Church showed the world a picture of something they couldn't live without? Right now, we portray legalism, misery and fear. What if we showed them the abundant life that comes with serving Christ? Would they be drawn to us? Would they be set free themselves? The lost cannot see a God who is being obscured by a Church that continually says, "Woe is me."

We lack abundance and settle for living a lower form of life. Only lavish generosity and love can truly represent heaven. Why are the most mean-spirited, tightfisted people found in church? How can we break that mindset once and for all?

When we have Christ in us, we can choose to see the possibilities of creating something wonderful in our life and circumstances. The life of Christ sets us free to be fully loved by heaven, and to participate in everything He wants to release into the earth.

> The life of Christ sets us free to be fully loved by heaven.

It's sad to think that many believers would rather fast and pray for a window to open in heaven than to perceive the simple truth that they are, in fact, that very window. How our thinking would change if we saw that we were the windows from heaven to earth!

When someone sees a branch full of fruit, they acknowledge the tree. "My, what a great apple tree," they say. Likewise, when people see Christians laden with abundance in God, they will acknowledge God. "To them God willed to make known what are the

riches of the glory of this mystery among the
Gentiles: which is Christ in you, the hope of glory,"
Paul wrote in Colossians 1:27.

A branch connected to a tree cannot deny the
strength of the trunk. Whatever is coursing through
the body of the tree flows into the branches. That
branch has to bear fruit—it has no choice. God
has given us the ability to create through our
thoughts. "As he thinks in his heart, so is he,"
Proverbs 23:7 puts it. What if we thought
differently about the world? What if we woke up
every day and centered our thoughts on the
possibility of what might occur when we reveal
more of the Kingdom of God to the people around
us? What if we went through the day looking for
the hand of God everywhere?

I believe such a follower of Christ would find
exactly what he or she is looking for. When we
look for the good in someone or something, we see
it. The problem is that the enemy has convinced us
to look for the bad in everything. We speak out
every bad thing we see, giving names to what the
enemy is doing. Meanwhile, the treasure of God,
hidden just beneath the surface, has gone
unnoticed.

## the open window

In Ephesians 3:14–21, Paul outlines what this window from heaven looks like:

> For this reason I bow my knees to the Father of our Lord Jesus Christ, from whom the whole family in heaven and earth is named, that He would grant you, according to the riches of His glory, to be strengthened with might through His Spirit in the inner man, that Christ may dwell in your hearts through faith; that you, being rooted and grounded in love, may be able to comprehend with all the saints what is the width and length and depth and height—to know the love of Christ which passes knowledge; that you may be filled with all the fullness of God.
>
> Now to Him who is able to do exceedingly abundantly above all that we ask or think, according to the power that works in us, to Him be glory in the church by Christ Jesus to all generations, forever and ever. Amen.

When we have a substandard view of the majesty of God, it is impossible to glorify Him properly. In fact, we actually detract from His glory when we do not fully embrace it. Paul said that we have a name both in heaven and on earth. People know me on earth by the name Graham Cooke. Not a bad name, but there is another name by which heaven calls me. My name in Christ is the same as Christ's. So is yours.

A major part of being a disciple of Christ involves learning to walk in His name. We must believe in His name, learn the power of His name, ask in His name, receive in His name and live in His name. One of the beautiful things about Jesus' name is that it includes the abundance of His life.

When someone introduces themselves as John Rockefeller, what springs to mind? Abundant wealth. Why? Because we recognize the name. If someone said, "I'm Bill Gates," what would come to our mind? *Mucho dinero*. Why? Because we recognize the name.

Christ's name is above all other names, and we share it because of His sacrifice. Life in the Spirit, then, is about learning to live in His name and not our own. As Christians, we have been all too content to live in our own name and not access our heavenly one.

God's identity and imprint are on each one of us. We don't have to do anything to earn something from God. He is in us, and we are in Him. We can access an abundant life when we allow the Holy

Spirit to touch our imaginations and lead us there. In our heavenly name, we are granted His glorious riches. We are made immeasurably strong in our truest selves. We can live a life that is powerful and overwhelming.

## children of revelation

When we become children of revelation, processing the lessons we learn in hiddenness, we open ourselves up to the truth of who God is and who we are called to be. The aspect of God's nature by which we are most enthralled is the very feature He is developing in our lives. As we open up to the truth of who God is for us, He comes and inhabits our faith.

We can be rooted and grounded in all of the laughter, love, affection and life that flow out of heaven. This is why hiddenness is so vital—it develops and refines our faith to the place where we can truly believe God in every circumstance. Anything less than that is not abundant life. As Paul said in

> We must be rooted in all of the laughter, love, affection and life that flow out of heaven.

Philippians 4:13: "I can do all things through Christ who strengthens me."

It's a simple principle: If we want the presence of God, we have to learn to be present with God. We have to open ourselves to His abundant life by searching out the depth, height, width and length of who God is for us. In manifestation, He will take us to the dizzying heights of His nature and show us His Kingdom's glory. In hiddenness, He will show us the depths of who He is, who we are and how our spirit can intermingle with His.

Hiddenness often takes us to the point of despair. We each have to come to a place where we despise ourselves and our sinful nature. At that darkest point, God looks at us and says, "I love you, just the way you are." In the moment of our greatest failure, we can be confident that God looks at us and says, "You are so beautiful to Me." This revelation of His tender and unshakable mercy breaks our heart and leads us to the point where we will never think the same way about ourselves again.

God wants us to come to a deeper understanding of Him and a new mindset about ourselves. He wants us to rethink where we fit into the majesty of heaven and the fullness of Christ.

Our role in this is not difficult. We are called to receive and remain within a life and love so vast that our mind does not have the capacity to fathom it. God's love ought to blow our minds. If it doesn't do this for you, you need to rethink your life. The abundant life God has given us is astonishing, amazing, astounding, wondrous, surprising, confounding, unfathomable and almost alarming in its scope and beauty.

Whenever God appeared to someone in Scripture, He always said three words: "Don't be afraid." Clearly, the beauty of God can be so overwhelming that it could kill us. He dwells in unapproachable light and yet beckons us to come and sit with Him. He's altogether wonderful. When He shows up, He is so dazzling that we don't know what to do with ourselves.

## the challenge of abundant life

When we are filled with the fullness of God, we are challenged by the Holy Spirit to share that abundant life with others on this earth. Walking with God pushes us to think beyond what seems possible, reasonable or even normal. He wants us to understand that He is able to do far more than we could ever ask.

God speaks to us in dreams and visions as a way to circumvent our inflexible thoughts about Him. He uses them to get us to explore a world full of possibility. In Scripture, we read of only one time when God allowed Himself to be put in a box—and He said if we touched it, He'd kill us! Our wildest dreams are not even close to the full measure of the power of God. The Pharisees, in Jesus' day, were dream thieves. They stole people's dreams about God and locked them up in a religious system that forced individuals to come to meetings and follow inane lists of "commandments" in order to be worthy of God's love.

> Your wildest dreams are not even close to the full measure of the power of God.

The Church should be about setting people free to absolutely adore Jesus, but often we fall into the same Pharisaical trap. When we really love God, we only want to do what we see Him doing. Our dream is to do the will of Him who saved us.

In Luke 4, Jesus read the prophecy of Isaiah 61, and claimed it as His "inheritance word": "The Spirit of the LORD is upon Me, because He has anointed Me to preach the gospel to the poor; He has sent Me to heal the brokenhearted, to proclaim liberty to the captives and recovery of sight to the blind, to set at liberty those who are oppressed" (verse 18). It is interesting to note that Jesus read this prophecy out loud in the church of His day, not among the people at the Sermon on the Mount. He obviously felt that people in the church of the day were just as imprisoned and lost as the people in the world.

How many of us are imprisoned by a system that is not guaranteed to set us free? It is the personal responsibility of every single one of us to pursue our own relationship with God. It is not the Church's job to give that to us, but our mission to find our unique place in Christ. It's time to be caught by Jesus again.

## caught by Jesus

We must be caught up by Jesus, to stop "doing" church and start "being" Church. We must learn to be followers of Jesus. We have to pursue friendship with God and one another. And we must chase God's abundance, not just for ourselves, but for everyone around us. The abundant life God gives us spills over

> When will we stop "doing" church and start "being" Church?

and positively changes the people we know and love. Everyone we meet should connect with our abundance, just as we connect with God's.

Jesus was not God pretending to be a man; He was fully, completely human. "Jesus of Nazareth, a

Man attested by God to you by miracles, wonders, and signs which God did through Him in your midst," said Peter on the Day of Pentecost (Acts 2:22). When Jesus told the disciples that He could do nothing apart from the power of God, He wasn't being humble—He was being honest. "Most assuredly, I say to you, the Son can do nothing of Himself, but what He sees the Father do; for whatever He does, the Son also does in like manner," Jesus said in John 5:19. That word, *nothing*, means exactly that: nothing. Jesus had no supernatural capability within Himself. It all flowed from an abundant life that He forged in an intimate relationship with His Father. He was fully God, yes, but He chose to live within the limitations of the people He came to redeem.

This is an important thing to understand because we have the same limitations and opportunities as Jesus. When we read the gospels and the book of Acts, we are reading our own story of abundant life. We can do all that—and more. We're reading about how to live in a limiting world with the limitless resources of the Kingdom of heaven at our disposal. We're learning how to abide in the Father, just as Jesus did. We're learning how to be wonderfully and creatively dependent on

God's generosity. We're learning how to dream outrageously.

If Jesus performed those miracles because He was God, then nothing is attainable for us. But if He did them as a man living in God, then we have a responsibility to pursue that lifestyle.

All it takes is spending time with God and adopting His mindset. When Jesus walked on water, He inspired Peter to ask to do the same. In that instant, Jesus didn't hand His friend a 45-minute sermon on how to walk on water. He didn't say, "Here's a great journal written by My friend, Graham Cooke." He didn't give him a website of resources to which he could log on. He grinned and said, "Come." In a flash, Peter was walking on a substance that he had no business standing on, except that he was full of abundant life.

We cannot be starved or dehydrated in the Spirit, because Jesus has promised us abundant life. He is our Bread and our Water—and a life that cannot be starved can feed everyone. This is our call and our privilege: to demonstrate a fruitful, abundant, full life to every human being on earth.

### A Prayer for Wisdom and Faith

Father, I thank You that I am the apple of Your eye.
I know that You seek to hide me in the secret place of Your
    presence.

Teach me how to abide in You,
To dwell and remain in Christ,
Hidden away in Your heart,
Safe from the hands of the enemy.

Help me to understand the wisdom of hiddenness,
To perceive the revelation of Your presence by wisdom and
    faith.

When my soul cries out for Your manifest presence,
May it hear the soothing words of the inner man of the Spirit,
Saying, *Peace! Be at rest. God is here.*

Raise up my inner man so that my soul capitulates to childlike
    trust, not emotion.
Teach me to see You by faith,
So that the reality of Your continuous presence remains with
    me at all times.

In Jesus' name,
Amen.

## A Psalm of Thanksgiving for Hiddenness

Father, I am so grateful to You
For the revelation of hiddenness.
Thank You that the increase of wisdom and faith
Is enabling me to behold You at all times.

Thank You that You never leave me, nor forsake me.
I worship Your kindness and goodness to me.
I see Your hand upon my life at this time.

Thank You for the power and purpose of Your Holy Spirit.
He will lead me into the full expression
Of Your truth in hiddenness.

Thank You, Father, that by Your grace
I will learn this spiritual discipline.
As I grow in Your wisdom, I will change internally
To become like You.

I will never again be at the mercy of external things or
     influences.
Instead, my inner man of the spirit will be able to access You
At all times and through all circumstances.

Thank You for teaching me this wonderful lesson.
Thank You for showing me another dimension of life in the
     Spirit.

I bless Your name.
Amen.

# meditation exercise

The following exercise is provided as an aid to assist you in spending time with God in the "hidden" place. Make sure that you allow adequate time to be still before the Lord and "quiet" any distracting thoughts. Follow the instructions below and write down what you sense the Lord is saying to you.

- ▶ Pray quietly for peace, stillness and rest.
- ▶ Speak the name of Jesus softly until your internal thoughts are relaxed.

1. What is the Lord saying to you?
   - Initially, write down only key words and phrases.
   - Now, put these thoughts into full sentences.
   - Arrange these sentences into a coherent order, and write yourself a letter as though it was written by God.

2.  What would you like to say to the Lord?
    - Initially, write down only key words and
      phrases.
    - Now, put these thoughts into full sentences.
    - Arrange these sentences into a coherent
      order, and write a letter to the Lord,
      expressing both thanksgiving and prayer.

3.  What is it that you are more fully able to
    understand about your relationship with God
    as a result of this exercise?

# assignment 1

▶ Think of a friend who may be struggling in his or her experience of God.

▶ Write on a card (using no more than 500 words) a specific word of encouragement that involves a Scripture and a childlike explanation of hiddenness.

▶ Mail it!

# assignment 2

Think of three people in your life at this time, including:

- ▶ A person whom you do not know well,
- ▶ A person to whom you find it difficult to relate, and
- ▶ A person with whom you are very familiar, but with whom you need to take your relationship to a deeper level.

From a place of hiddenness, close to the heart of God, ask for wisdom to see each person the way that God sees them.

> Finally, brethren, whatever things are true, whatever things are noble, whatever things are just, whatever things are pure, whatever things are lovely,

whatever things are of good report, if there is any
virtue and if there is anything praiseworthy—
meditate on these things.

Philippians 4:8

Write a card to each of these people, providing
specific encouragement as you declare to them how
the Lord sees them.

# assignment 3

## Lectio Divina

*Lectio Divina* (Latin for "divine reading") is an ancient way of reading the Bible—allowing a quiet and contemplative way of coming to God's Word. *Lectio Divina* opens the pulse of the Scriptures, helping readers dig far deeper into the Word than normally happens in a quick glance-over.

In this exercise, we will look at a portion of Scripture and use a modified *Lectio Divina* technique to engage with it. This technique can be used on any passage of Scripture; I highly recommend using it for key Bible passages that the Lord has highlighted for you, and for anything you think might be an "inheritance word" for your life (see *The Crafted Prayer Interactive Journal* for more on inheritance words).

Now behold, two of them were traveling that same day to a village called Emmaus, which was seven miles from Jerusalem. And they talked together of all these things which had happened. So it was, while they conversed and reasoned, that Jesus Himself drew near and went with them. But their eyes were restrained, so that they did not know Him.

And He said to them, "What kind of conversation is this that you have with one another as you walk and are sad?"

Then the one whose name was Cleopas answered and said to Him, "Are You the only stranger in Jerusalem, and have You not known the things which happened there in these days?"

And He said to them, "What things?"

So they said to Him, "The things concerning Jesus of Nazareth, who was a Prophet mighty in deed and word before God and all the people, and how the chief priests and our rulers delivered Him to be condemned to death, and crucified Him. But we were hoping that it was He who was going to redeem Israel. Indeed, besides all this, today is the third day since these things happened. Yes, and certain women of our company, who arrived at the tomb early, astonished us. When they did not find His body, they came saying that they had also seen a vision of angels who said He was alive. And certain of those who were with us went to the tomb and found it just as the women had said; but Him they did not see."

Then He said to them, "O foolish ones, and slow of heart to believe in all that the prophets have spoken! Ought not the Christ to have suffered these things and to enter into His glory?" And beginning at Moses and all the Prophets, He expounded to them in all the Scriptures the things concerning Himself.

Then they drew near to the village where they were going, and He indicated that He would have gone farther. But they constrained Him, saying, "Abide with us, for it is toward evening, and the day is far spent." And He went in to stay with them.

Now it came to pass, as He sat at the table with them, that He took bread, blessed and broke it, and gave it to them. Then their eyes were opened and they knew Him; and He vanished from their sight.

Luke 24:13–31

1.  Find a place of stillness before God. Embrace His peace. Calm your body, breathe slowly ... clear your mind of the distractions of life. Ask God to reveal His rest to you. Whisper the word, *"Stillness."* This can take some time, but once you're in that place of rest, enjoy it. Worship God out of it.

2. Read the passage twice, slowly.
   a. Allow its words to become familiar to you, and sink into your spirit. Picture the scene— become part of it. Listen for pieces that catch your attention.
   b. Following the reading, meditate upon what you have heard. What stands out? Write it down.

   . . . . . . . . . . . . . . . . . . . . . . . . . . . . . . . . . . . . .
   . . . . . . . . . . . . . . . . . . . . . . . . . . . . . . . . . . . . .
   . . . . . . . . . . . . . . . . . . . . . . . . . . . . . . . . . . . . .

   c. If a word or phrase from the passage seems highlighted to you, write it down.

   . . . . . . . . . . . . . . . . . . . . . . . . . . . . . . . . . . . . .
   . . . . . . . . . . . . . . . . . . . . . . . . . . . . . . . . . . . . .
   . . . . . . . . . . . . . . . . . . . . . . . . . . . . . . . . . . . . .

3. Read the passage twice, again.
   a. Like waves crashing onto a shore, let the words of the Scripture crash onto your spirit. What are you discerning? What are you hearing? What are you feeling? Write it down.

   . . . . . . . . . . . . . . . . . . . . . . . . . . . . . . . . . . . . .
   . . . . . . . . . . . . . . . . . . . . . . . . . . . . . . . . . . . . .
   . . . . . . . . . . . . . . . . . . . . . . . . . . . . . . . . . . . . .
   . . . . . . . . . . . . . . . . . . . . . . . . . . . . . . . . . . . . .

b. What is the theme of this passage? Write it down.

. . . . . . . . . . . . . . . . . . . . . . . . . . . . . . . . . . . . . .
. . . . . . . . . . . . . . . . . . . . . . . . . . . . . . . . . . . . . .
. . . . . . . . . . . . . . . . . . . . . . . . . . . . . . . . . . . . . .

c. Does this passage rekindle any memories or experiences? Write them down.

. . . . . . . . . . . . . . . . . . . . . . . . . . . . . . . . . . . . . .
. . . . . . . . . . . . . . . . . . . . . . . . . . . . . . . . . . . . . .
. . . . . . . . . . . . . . . . . . . . . . . . . . . . . . . . . . . . . .
. . . . . . . . . . . . . . . . . . . . . . . . . . . . . . . . . . . . . .

d. What is the Holy Spirit saying to you? Write it down.

. . . . . . . . . . . . . . . . . . . . . . . . . . . . . . . . . . . . . .
. . . . . . . . . . . . . . . . . . . . . . . . . . . . . . . . . . . . . .
. . . . . . . . . . . . . . . . . . . . . . . . . . . . . . . . . . . . . .
. . . . . . . . . . . . . . . . . . . . . . . . . . . . . . . . . . . . . .

4. Read the passage two final times.
   a. Meditate on it.
   b. Is there something God wants you to do with this passage? Is there something to which He is calling you? Write it down.

. . . . . . . . . . . . . . . . . . . . . . . . . . . . . . . . . . . . . .
. . . . . . . . . . . . . . . . . . . . . . . . . . . . . . . . . . . . . .
. . . . . . . . . . . . . . . . . . . . . . . . . . . . . . . . . . . . . .
. . . . . . . . . . . . . . . . . . . . . . . . . . . . . . . . . . . . . .

c. Pray silently. Tell God the thoughts this Scripture is bringing to your mind. Ask Him for His thoughts. Write down your conversation—as if you and God were sitting in a coffee shop, two old and dear friends, sharing.

. . . . . . . . . . . . . . . . . . . . . . . . . . . . . . . . . . . .

. . . . . . . . . . . . . . . . . . . . . . . . . . . . . . . . . . . .

. . . . . . . . . . . . . . . . . . . . . . . . . . . . . . . . . . . .

. . . . . . . . . . . . . . . . . . . . . . . . . . . . . . . . . . . .

. . . . . . . . . . . . . . . . . . . . . . . . . . . . . . . . . . . .

. . . . . . . . . . . . . . . . . . . . . . . . . . . . . . . . . . . .

5. Pray and thank God for what He has shared with you. Come back to the passage a few more times over the coming weeks.

# FAQs
## (frequently asked questions)

Q.   *Who is Graham Cooke, and how can I find more information about him?*

A.   Graham Cooke is a speaker and author who splits his time between Southampton, England, and Vacaville, California. He has been involved in prophetic ministry since 1974. He founded and directed the School of Prophecy, which has received international acclaim for its advanced series of in-depth training programs. Graham is a member of Community Church in Southampton (UK).

He is married to Heather, and they have three children: Ben, Seth and Sophie. You can learn more about Graham at:

www.grahamcooke.com

or by writing him at:

P.O. Box 91
Southampton
England SO15 57E

Q.   *How can I become a prayer partner with Graham?*

A.   Check his website, www.grahamcooke.com, for all of the information you need.

Q.   *Has Graham written any other books?*

A.   Graham has written several other books: *A Divine Confrontation: Birth Pangs of the New Church* (Destiny Image), *Developing Your Prophetic Gifting* (Chosen), *Crafted Prayer* (Chosen), *Drawing Close* (Chosen), *God Revealed* (Chosen), *The Language of Love* (Chosen) and *The Secret of a Powerful Inner Life* (Chosen). All are available at most Christian bookstores or at www.grahamcooke.com.

# about the author

Graham Cooke is married to Heather, and they have
three adult children: Ben, Seth and Sophie. Graham
and Heather divide their time between Southampton,
England, and Vacaville, California.

Graham is a member of Community Church in
Southampton (UK), responsible for the prophetic and
training program, and working with team leader
Billy Kennedy. In California, he is part of the
pastoral leadership team, working with senior pastor
David Crone. He has responsibility for Insight, a
training program within the church and for the
region.

Graham is a popular conference speaker and is
well known for his training programs on the
prophetic, spiritual warfare, intimacy with God,
leadership and spirituality. He functions as a
consultant, specifically helping churches make the
transition from one dimension of calling to a higher
level of vision and ministry. He has a passion to
build prototype churches that can fully reach our
postmodern society.

A strong part of Graham's ministry is in producing finances and resources to help the poor, supporting many projects around the world. He also financially supports and helps to underwrite church planting, leadership development, evangelism and health and rescue projects in the third world. If you wish to become a financial partner for the sake of missions, please contact Graham's office, where his personal assistant, Carole Shiers, will be able to assist you.

Graham has many prayer partners who play a significant part in his ministry. For more information, check his website.

Contact details for Graham Cooke:

▶ **United States:**
Vaca Valley Christian Life Center
6391 Leisure Town Road
Vacaville
CA 95687

email: fti.admin@vvclc.org

▶ **United Kingdom:**
Sword of Fire Ministries
P.O. Box 1
Southampton SO16 7WJ

email: admin@swordfire.org.uk

▶ **Canada:**
Jenny Bateman
Friends Langley Vineyard
5708 Glover Road
Langley
BC V3A 4H8

email: jenn@shopvineyard.com

▶ website: www.grahamcooke.com